DOGS&CATS

DOMESTIC ANIMAL BOOKS FOR KIDS

Children's Animal Books

Speedy Publishing LLC

40 E. Main St. #1156

Newark, DE 19711

www.speedypublishing.com

Dogs and cats have lived with people for a very long time. They are among the first animals that became *"Domesticated"*, so they became comfortable living with humans. Dogs and cats are our most favorite pets. Let's find out why!

Puppy with tabby cat.

OUR FAVORITE PETS

In the United States, there are over seventy-seven million cats and fifty-five million dogs who live with humans, in about 75 million homes. The vast majority are family pets, although there are some dogs who work with police forces or on farms. Cats are a little more reluctant to work for their living, but you do sometimes see them dozing in the windows of small stores, keeping the owner company.

Cats and dogs are complicated and interesting animals. Here are some differences between them:

- Cats can make about one hundred different mouth noises (vocalizations) to communicate, from hisses and yowls to purrs. Dogs are limited to about ten.

- Dogs can learn tasks, tricks, and commands very quickly, sometimes in just a few minutes. These can range from "Sit" and "Roll over" to the more complicated tasks that assistance dogs have to learn so they can help their disabled owners. Cats, on the other hand, are very difficult to train: they don't seem to see the point of doing what you want them to do!

- Dogs can take a long time to be house-trained, so they know not to make a mess in the house. Cats are instinctively house-trained: if you make a litter box available, they will use it.

- Dogs are pack animals: they like to be with others. A dog in a family will consider the family members as part of its pack and will want to hang out with them. Cats are more solitary. They tend to be more attached to their territory than to the people or other pets who share it with them.

- Dogs have 42 teeth, while cats have 30.

- Cats have three times as many scent receptors in their noses as people do—but dogs have 14 times as many!

- Cats are good at jumping and climbing, so they can hunt in more places for food and get away from danger more easily. Dogs can jump, but they are not good climbers.

- Dogs are scavenging meat-eaters, which means that while they prefer meat, they can survive when only plant material is available. Cats are strict meat-eaters. They cannot survive on a diet that has no fish or meat.

- Wild dogs hunt by chasing their prey and wearing it out. They can run long distances, so even if what they want to catch is faster at first, if the dogs can keep it running and not going up into trees or down into a burrow, they can tire it out. Cats hunt by sneaking up on their prey and then pouncing. They can run fast over short distance, but they don't run long distances.

- Cats see the same range of colors that humans do, but dogs have a narrower color range. Dogs' color range includes blue, green, yellow, and shades of gray.

- Cat claws stay sharp because they can retract them into their paws when they don't need to use them. Dog claws are always exposed, so they get worn down by contact with the ground and other objects.

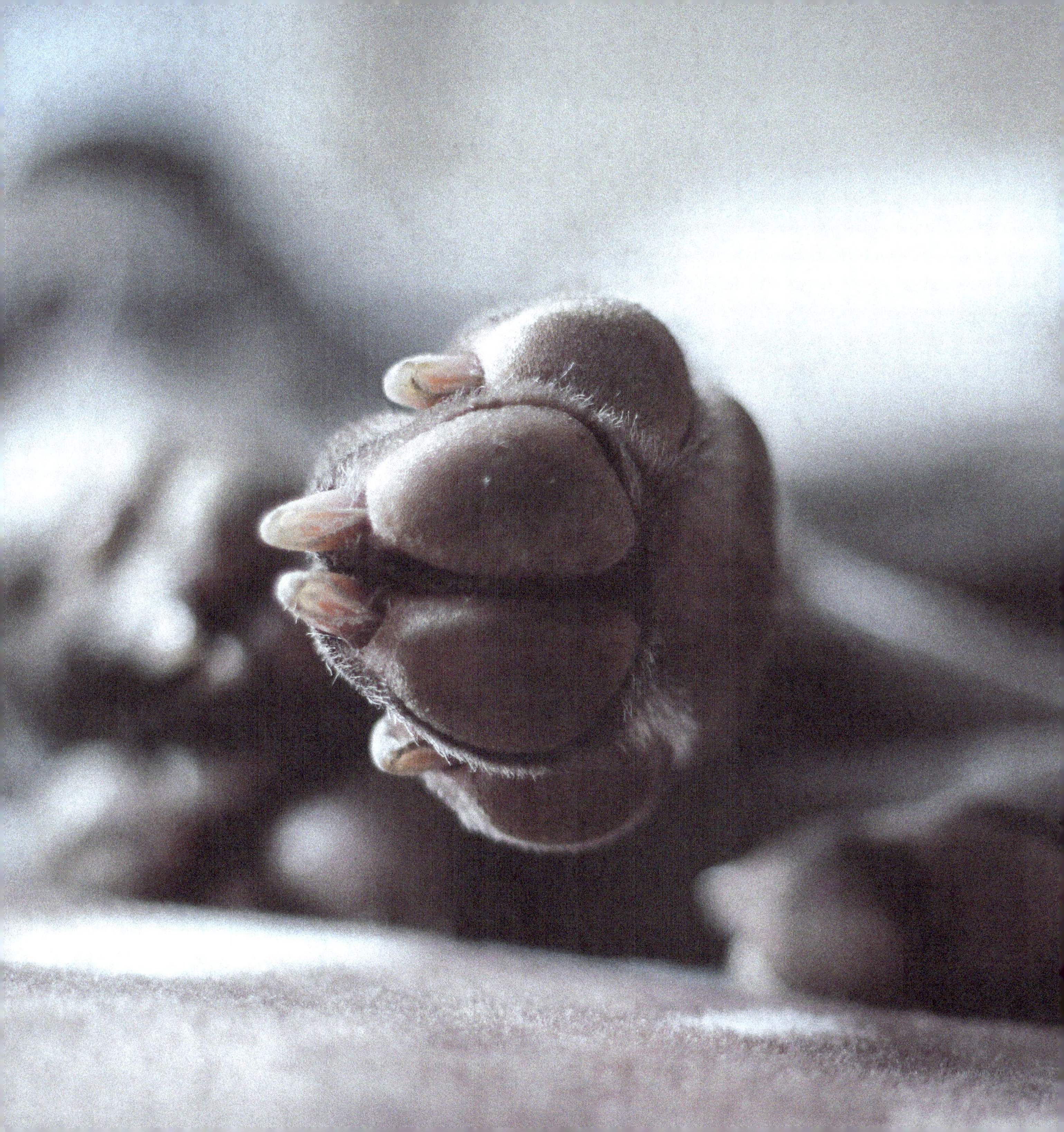

- While humans have about nine thousand taste buds on their tongues, dogs have only about 1,700. Cats are even more limited, with fewer than 500.

Cat Paw.

And here are two ways that cats and dogs are alike:

- Every cat and dog's nose is unique, the way your fingerprints are unique. You can take a "nose-print" of your cat or dog so you can identify it later if it gets lost or is stolen.

- Chocolate is like poison for both cats and dogs.

MAN'S BEST FRIEND

Dogs have been living and working with people since we lived in caves. They have hunted with us and guarded our sheep and cattle. In modern times dogs work as guides for blind people, as guard dogs, pulling sleds, herding sheep and cattle, as officers in the police force and border patrol, as rescue dogs, using their strong sense of smell to track people, and as therapy dogs to help people who are very sad, very lonely, or troubled in other ways.

Here are more things to know about dogs:

- Dogs like pugs, boxers, and bulldogs have flatter faces with shorter noses and jaws. This makes them more likely to have breathing and dental problems, among other ailments.

- All dalmations are born completely white. After a few weeks they develop their spots.

- Dogs only have sweat glands on their feet. The way they get rid of heat their body does not need is by panting.

Pug Puppy.

- Dogs' noses are wet to help them smell better. The wetness collects more scent particles out of the air.

- Dogs are so closely related to wolves that a wolf and a dog can mate and have offspring.

Dalmatian puppy.

- Dogs use eighteen muscles to move their ears. This means they can focus precisely on where a noise is coming from. This also means they can change their facial expressions subtly to communicate emotions ranging from curiosity to excitement to fear to sadness.

Pit Bull.

- Dogs chase their tails for exercise, when they are anxious, when they get confused and think their tail is a little animal they might like to eat, or when fleas are biting their tail.

- Dogs have dreams the same way people do. When you see a dog sort of twitching and running in its sleep, it is probably dreaming about chasing a rabbit!

- Dogs' eyes have a special membrane, the tapetum lucidem, that helps them see well even in the dark.

- Along with the membrane, a dog's eye has three eyelids: an upper and lower lid, and a clear third lid called a *"Haw"* or *"Nictitating Membrane"*. The haw keeps the eye moist and protects it from dust and other objects.

- Almost half of dogs who are household pets sleep on their owner's bed.

Collie.

- The higher-pitched the sound, the better dogs can hear it. That's why some dog owners use whistles pitched so high that most humans can't hear them at all. Humans hear sound frequencies best around 2000 Hertz (Hz), while dogs hear best at 8,000 Hz.

- After dogs relieve themselves, they often kick at the ground. They are not trying to bury what they just did: they are marking their territory by using the scent glands in their paws.

Kitten.

PURRFECT

In Rudyard Kipling's story *"The Cat That Walked by Himself"*, a cat comes to live with a family living in a cave, tens of thousands of years ago. In exchange for food and a place by the fire, the cat agrees to purr for the baby so the baby won't cry.

That is a made-up story that describes how cats and humans get along. Cats are far more independent than dogs, but they make a connection with certain humans and in exchange for food and shelter will entertain them or sleep in their laps to keep them from getting up and working!

Here are some things to know about cats:

- Cow milk is not good for cats.

- A kitten is not born knowing how to hunt. If its parent or another cat doesn't teach the kitten, it may never figure it out.

- House cats sleep about sixteen hours a day. Their cousins, the tigers and lions and other wild hunters, sleep even longer every day. The only other species that averages more time asleep every day is the sloth!

- Most female cats prefer using their right paws, and most male cats tend to use their left paws when they have a choice.

- All cats have blue eyes when they are born. They slowly get their true eye color a couple of weeks after birth.

- Cats hiss and yowl at other cats, and purr at their kittens, but they don't meow at them. They save meowing for when they have to ask humans for something.

- A cat can jump into the air about seven times its height.

- If a cat can get its head into an opening, it can probably get the rest of its body through, too. The design of its shoulders lets the cat make itself narrow when squeezing through narrow places.

- When a cat walks, its left legs move together and its right legs move together. Only cats, giraffes, and camels have this way of walking.

Learn more about the wild ancestors of domestic cats in the Baby Professor book My Pet Cat Has Wild Cousins.

British Shorthair Cat.

LEARN MORE ABOUT THE WORLD'S ANIMALS!

Whether they share a home with us or live in the wild world, animals are fascinating! Read other Baby Professor books, like *Who Lives in the Barren Desert?, The Great White Shark, The Endangered Mammals from Around the World,* and *How do Animals Help the Forest Grow?,* to learn even more!

Visit
BABY PROFESSOR
EDUCATION KIDS
www.BabyProfessorBooks.com
to download Free Baby Professor eBooks
and view our catalog of new and exciting
Children's Books

www.ingramcontent.com/pod-product-compliance
Lightning Source LLC
Chambersburg PA
CBHW060614120726

48002CB00010B/2960